W.K. Kellogg

Community BUILDERS

W.K. Kellogg

Community BUILDERS

Generous Genius

by
Rachel Epstein

Children's Press®
A Division of Grolier Publishing
New York / London / Hong Kong / Sydney
Danbury, Connecticut

Photo Credits

Photographs ©: Archive Photos: 11, 31; Brown Brothers: 8, 17, 18, 19; Corbis-Bettmann: 21 (UPI), cover, 27 top; Envision: 24 (Steven Needham); Liaison Agency, Inc.: 27 bottom, 33 (Giboux), back cover (Porter Gifford), 6 bottom (James Kozyra), 44 (Charlie Westerman); Photos provided by the W. K. Kellogg Foundation: 2, 3, 6 top, 9, 12, 14, 15 top, 16, 22, 30, 34, 35, 36, 39, 41, 42; Compliment of Kellogg Company: 15 bottom.

Visit Children's Press on the Internet at:
http://publishing.grolier.com

Library of Congress Cataloging-in-Publication Data

Epstein, Rachel
    W. K. Kellogg : generous genius / Rachel Epstein.
       p. cm. — (Community builders)
    Includes bibliographical references and index.
    Summary: A biography of the man who founded the successful cereal empire and established the second-largest charitable foundation in the United States.
    ISBN: 0-516-21605-8 (lib.bdg.)
    1. Kellogg, W. K. (Will Keith), 1860–1951—Juvenile literature. 2. Industrialists—United States—Biography—Juvenile literature. 3. Philanthropists—United States—Biography—Juvenile literature. 4. Kellogg Company—History—Juvenile literature. 5. W. K. Kellogg Foundation—History—Juvenile literature. 7. Battle Creek (Mich.)—Biography—Juvenile literature. [1. Kellogg, W. K. (Will Keith), 1860–1951. 2. Industrialists. 3. Philanthropists.] I. Title. II. Series.
HD9056.U45 K453   2000
338.7'6647'092—dc21
[B]   99-059779

©2000 Children's Press®, a Division of Grolier Publishing Co., Inc.
All rights reserved. Published simultaneously in Canada.
Printed in the United States of America.
1 2 3 4 5 6 7 8 9 10 R 09 08 07 06 05 04 03 02 01 00

Contents

**Above: W. K. Kellogg
at the age of forty
Right: Millions of bowls
of cereal are eaten
for breakfast each day.**

Chapter ONE

Behind the Cereal Box

If you had cereal for breakfast this morning, the chances are good that the name Kellogg was on the box. This is true whether you ate Sugar Frosted Flakes® or Corn Flakes™, Rice Krispies® or Special K®, Kellogg's Smacks® or Cracklin' Oat Bran®. And it would also have been true for your parents when they were young and for their parents and their parents, going all the way back to when W. K. Kellogg founded his cereal company in 1906.

When W. K. Kellogg started his company, it was one of forty-two companies that would make cereal in Battle Creek, a small town in Michigan. Most of those other companies lasted only a short time. One

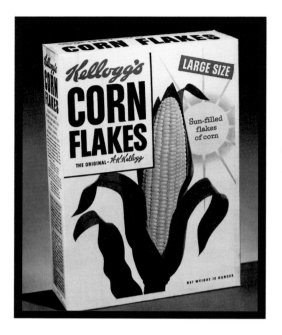

Kellogg's cereal was discovered by accident in 1906.

reason that Kellogg's company lasted is that he thought big. While one of his workers dreamed of selling cases of cereal through catalogs to people who had visited Battle Creek, W. K. Kellogg dreamed of selling trainloads of hundreds of thousands of cases of cereal to people all over the world.

The man whose name is on all those cereal boxes did not at first seem likely to succeed. He was poor and not a good student. For many years, he worked for his older brother, a famous doctor, who thought he was a "loafer."

8

While W. K. Kellogg did not even start his own company until he was forty-six years old, he turned out to have a great mind for business. From the success of his cereal company, W. K. Kellogg was able to live a comfortable life and still give away millions of dollars to improve the lives of other people.

With his fortune, Kellogg was able to improve the health of poor children.

Chapter TWO

Early Life

Will Keith Kellogg's ancestors came to the Massachusetts-Connecticut area of North America from England in the mid-1600s. His father, John Preston Kellogg, ran a ferry across the Connecticut River in Massachusetts. He was also a farmer. Life was hard for the Kellogg family, and they went west in 1834. Kellogg's father had heard that there was better land for farming in the wild and undeveloped part of the United States called the Michigan Territory. The family traveled by horse-drawn wagon on a rough road between forests of tall trees and also took boats to get to their new home.

A few years after the family arrived in Michigan, John's first wife, Mary Ann Kellogg, died of

**Like the Kelloggs, many families headed
west in hopes of a better life.**

tuberculosis. Tuberculosis is an infection caused by
bacteria, and it usually affects a person's lungs. It is
especially common in people who are undernour-
ished or overworked.

Several months after his wife died, John Preston
Kellogg married Ann Janette Stanley, who was to
become W. K. Kellogg's mother. Their daughter

Battle Creek's Main Street in 1868

Emma died in 1849 as a young girl. After the death of their daughter, the Kelloggs became interested in a new religion called Seventh-day Adventism. Adventist preachers talked about the benefits of living a healthy life. In 1856, the Adventists established their headquarters in Battle Creek,

12

partly because people in Michigan, unlike people in some other parts of the country, were open to those with different beliefs. Soon after John Preston Kellogg moved to Battle Creek, he gave up farming and opened a broom factory that he thought would give him more money to contribute to the church.

Seventh-day Adventism

Seventh-day Adventism is a Protestant Christian religion that believes Christ will soon return to earth. Adventists hold their religious services on the seventh day, or Saturday. They are encouraged to lead healthy lives by exercising, getting enough rest, eating well, and avoiding alcohol and tobacco products.

Kellogg was born on April 7, 1860, in this house.

Will Keith Kellogg was born on April 7, 1860. Will Keith's mother had good ideas about how to make money, and she was generous to her neighbors. But she and her husband were so serious that when W. K. Kellogg looked back on his childhood, he said he "never learned to play."

14

Kellogg at fourteen

Young Will Keith began working at the age of seven, making brooms in his father's factory and growing vegetables in the family gardens. He left school at the age of fourteen to become a full-time broom salesman. One reason Will Keith was happy to leave school is that his teacher thought he was a bad student. The real problem, however, was that his eyesight was bad and he could not see the blackboard.

While he may not have been a good student, Will Keith Kellogg had strong business skills. In fact, Will Keith was such a good manager that the Seventh-day Adventist Church sent him to Texas to manage a broom factory when he was only nineteen.

Kellogg working as a broom salesman

Ella Osborn Davis

After a successful year in Texas, Will Keith Kellogg moved back to Battle Creek. He married his hometown sweetheart, Ella Osborn Davis, in 1880. They had four sons and a daughter, but one of their sons died as an infant and another son died at the age of four. Will Keith was a stern father, insisting that his children call him "Sir," which was not unusual in his day. He also worked such long hours for his brother that he left the house before his children were awake and returned home after they were asleep.

16

Chapter THREE

Working at the Sanitarium

When he was twenty years old, W. K. Kellogg went to work for his older brother, Dr. John Harvey Kellogg, at the Battle Creek Sanitarium, nicknamed the "San." The San was a combination of a hospital and a resort run by the Seventh-day Adventists.

Dr. John Harvey Kellogg

Patients at the San taking a morning sun bath

The medical treatments at the San were different from the typical medicine in the 1800s. This was a time when doctors did not know about the importance of germs in spreading disease and were just beginning to learn that clean living conditions were important to health. There were no antibiotics (a type of medicine that helps to fight

The men's bath area at the San

off diseases). If people needed surgery, it was extremely painful because there were no anesthetics, which are drugs that reduce pain. At the San, the emphasis was on natural methods of preventing and curing illnesses—rest, exercise, sunshine, and simple food. The San did not serve tea, coffee, liquor, meat, or spicy food.

An important feature of life at the San was hydrotherapy, or water therapy, which offered many types of showers and baths. The Adventists believed that water was "God's great medicine." They believed that enough water inside and outside the body would draw a person's illness to the surface. From the surface, the illness would leave the person's body and let him be healthy again.

John Harvey Kellogg was a brilliant doctor with a lot of energy. He traveled around the world to learn the latest methods of diagnosis and treatment of illnesses. He understood the harmful effects of smoking long before the connection between cancer and cigarettes was generally accepted.

W. K. Kellogg's work at the San, however, was much less exciting than his brother's. He described himself as a "bookkeeper, cashier, packing and shipping clerk, errand boy, and general utility man" and said he even shaved his brother and shined his shoes. If people ran away, he went to bring them back. And if someone died, W. K. Kellogg went with the family to select the casket. He also figured out

Dr. Kellogg meets with writer George Bernard Shaw.

the prices that people paid to stay at the San and the additional prices for the books and foods the San sold. He also had to decide who would be admitted and who would get special rates or free treatment. He found it painful to have to choose which crippled, blind, or deaf poor people would get the San's services for free and who would be turned down. W. K. found it especially hard deciding which of the sick poor children would receive treatment.

W. K. Kellogg worried that he would never achieve success.

He worked long hours, but his brother did not appreciate him, paid him poorly, and called him a "loafer." Not surprisingly, W. K. Kellogg rarely smiled or laughed, and in 1884, he wrote in his diary, "I feel kind of blue. Am afraid that I will always be a poor man the way things look now."

Chapter FOUR

Creation of the Corn Flake

Corn flakes, which were the first product of W. K. Kellogg's cereal company, were the result of a lucky accident. But it was not an accident that the Kelloggs were trying to change the way many Americans ate. At the end of the 1800s, a typical breakfast in the United States was meat or fried eggs, fried potatoes, bread soaked in molasses, cornmeal, pie, and coffee. These were the same foods people might eat again at lunch and dinner. Food made especially for breakfast did not exist yet.

23

This large amount of heavy food was fine when most people did hard physical work like farming, mining for coal, or building railroads. However, by the beginning of the 1900s, people were doing less active work, and so much heavy food was making them sick. One of John Harvey Kellogg's discoveries, along with the dangers of smoking, was that eating fewer calories, or lighter food, helped people remain healthy.

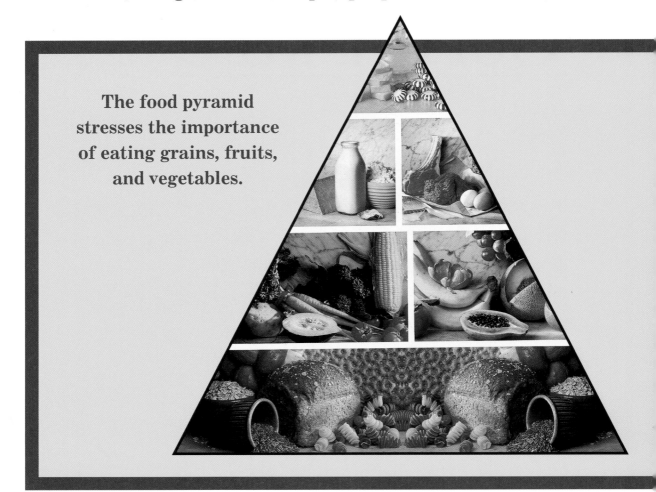

The food pyramid stresses the importance of eating grains, fruits, and vegetables.

Because John Harvey Kellogg thought spices were not healthful, the food at the San was often tasteless. This meant people would leave the San before their treatments were over or sneak out to restaurants in Battle Creek to get away from the San's cooking. To solve this problem, the San's kitchen tried to develop food, such as peanut butter, that would be both tasty and healthful.

Nutritional Standards

For good health, the U.S. Government recommends that you eat a variety of foods including a lot of grain products, vegetables, and fruits. The government also recommends only small amounts of sugar, salt, fat, and alcoholic beverages. You should also balance the food you eat with exercise. A good breakfast is part of healthy eating. Studies show that students who eat breakfast perform better in class.

In the early 1880s, John Harvey Kellogg started a new business called the Sanitas Food Company so that he could do more experimenting with food products. W. K. Kellogg also worked for him there. It was at this food company that the accidental discovery of the corn flake took place.

The discovery came in 1894, while the brothers were trying to make a bread that would be easy to digest. They made a big batch of wheat porridge. Instead of running the porridge through the big rollers that would chop it into tiny bits to be baked into bread, as they usually did, they were busy with other work and let the mushy stuff stay in the pot a few days. When they came back into the kitchen, the brothers saw that the wheat mixture was kind of spoiled, but they ran it through the rollers anyway. To their surprise, large, thin flakes emerged from the rollers. They then tried baking these new flakes. The flakes were crisp and flavorful, even without spices and even with the slightly spoiled flavor of the mixture. Letting wheat mush sit for a few days became the key to

Above: The original building where Kellogg's Corn Flakes were first produced

Left: An exhibit of the Kellogg brothers discovering the corn flake at Cereal City, USA

a whole new industry: breakfast food. In a few years, W.K. Kellogg learned that the flakes were even tastier if they were made with corn instead of wheat.

By 1903, W. K. Kellogg realized that the cereal flakes could make Sanitas into a large and profitable company. At first, the company's products were advertised only to patients who were at the San or had visited the San. But W. K. began advertising in publications read by people who wanted to live healthful lives, but who had never visited Battle Creek. These advertisements were bringing in many new customers. W. K. Kellogg also realized that adding a small amount of sugar to the cereal would make it taste even better. But his brother, John Harvey Kellogg, objected to these new business tactics. He thought that big advertising campaigns would hurt the sanitarium's medical reputation. He also was strongly against adding sugar to the cereal. It was time for W. K. Kellogg to make a decision.

Chapter FIVE

Building the Kellogg Company

W. K. Kellogg had spent twenty-five years doing what his brother wanted. In 1906, at the age of forty-six, he broke free and started the Battle Creek Toasted Corn Flake Company. With W. K. Kellogg's name appearing on every cereal box, the company was soon known as Kellogg's. W. K. believed that his new business would thrive. He wrote to a friend: "I sort of feel it in my bones that we are now preparing for a campaign on a food

Kellogg liked to visit his factory several times a week.

which will eventually prove to be the leading cereal of the United States, if not of the world."

To make his cereal a success, W. K. Kellogg used his natural instinct for business. There were more healthy people than sick people, so he decided that the advertising for cereal should emphasize its delicious taste as a breakfast food rather than its health benefits. Almost immediately, he took out a full-page ad in the July issue of The Ladies Home Journal, which was then one of the most popular magazines for women. This was a bold step for a new company, but the ad itself was even bolder.

The Ladies Home Journal ad told readers that more people wanted Kellogg's Corn Flakes than the factory could satisfy right now. It went on to say that the company soon expected to be able to fill its orders and offered a coupon for a whole season's worth of free Kellogg's Corn Flakes to any customer who asked a grocery store to stock the new product. It was unusual to advertise a product that was not available, to be so honest, and to ask shoppers to ask their grocers to buy a particular product.

The famous Kellogg ad from 1906

Kellogg also made good use of electric signs. In Chicago, an enormous neon-lit boy cried unhappily, and he was saying, "I want Kellogg's." A few seconds later, the sign changed to show the same boy with a smiling face saying, "I got Kellogg's." In hard economic times, when many companies decided to save money by stopping advertising, Kellogg increased the amount of money he spent on advertising. His gamble paid off in much higher sales.

Another way W. K. Kellogg was a good businessman was that he treated his workers well. On July 4, 1907, a fire burned the factory to the ground. Kellogg told his workers that they would all keep their jobs and that he wanted them there the next day to help with cleanup and construction. He liked to hire people with large families because then he knew their families would be supported. He also built inexpensive housing for his workers and provided them with entertainment, including sponsorship of a baseball team. If he heard that a worker was having trouble paying for a doctor or food, he would pay the bill himself and try to keep his generosity a secret.

Radio and Television Advertising

Kellogg was a major advertiser first on radio and then on television, sponsoring both Superman and Howdy Doody shows. Tony the Tiger™ has been growling "Sugar Frosted Flakes are gr-r-reat" since 1952.

The popular puppet, Howdy Doody, starred in its own television show from 1947 to 1960.

Tony the Tiger™ has been appearing in Kellogg's Frosted Flakes commercials for more than forty years.

While Kellogg was generous to his workers, he also had high expectations of them. He worked hard and did not believe in unnecessary expenses. He expected his employees to behave the same way.

In 1912, only six years after founding his cereal company, W. K. Kellogg became a millionaire. Along with great success, however, Kellogg suffered a personal loss that same year when his wife Ella died. Six years later, when he was fifty-eight years old, Kellogg married Dr. Carrie Staines.

W. K. and Carrie Kellogg

**W. K. Kellogg
with one
of his horses**

By 1925, Kellogg was wealthier than he ever imagined, owning enormous homes in Michigan and in California. At his home in California, he was able to fulfill a childhood dream of raising Arabian horses.

Kellogg celebrated his sixty-fifth birthday in 1925 with gifts to his hometown of Battle Creek. He provided the community with an auditorium, a junior high school, and a large recreation center for young people. He also gave money to improve the local farmer's market and donated land for a Boy Scout camp.

One of the many gifts that Kellogg gave Battle
Creek—a junior high and auditorium

Kellogg continued to be generous to his community. He gave a sanctuary where birds would be safe from hunters and a farm for experimenting with different plants and ways of plowing. And he developed a forest project that showed people how to farm on land that was once considered too poor for good farming.

Even when many other businesses faced tough times, Kellogg used his business to find ways to help people. During the economic Depression of the 1930s when millions of Americans lost their jobs, Kellogg's was the first company to work with four six-hour shifts per day instead of three eight-hour shifts per day, which meant that more people would have jobs. When he built a beautiful park next to the factory, he had the work done by hand rather than by machine. This meant a larger number of people were put to work.

In 1930, W. K. Kellogg established a foundation for "the promotion of the health, education and welfare of mankind, but principally of children and youth . . . without regard to sex, race, creed or nationality . . . ." Kellogg especially wanted "to help people to help themselves." The foundation received money directly from Kellogg and also from ownership of stock in Kellogg's company, which he donated. Today the Kellogg Foundation is one of the largest charitable foundations in the United States.

Ann J. Kellogg School

Founded in 1930 by W. K. Kellogg and named for his mother, the Ann J. Kellogg School was the first in the country to put children with difficulty moving, seeing, hearing, and learning into the same school with children who did those things easily. The school had an auditorium with spaces for wheelchairs, a water therapy pool, carpeting on many surfaces so children with hearing problems were not be distracted by unnecessary noises, and machines that translated books into Braille so blind children could read.

In the 1930s, the W. K. Kellogg Foundation started the Michigan Community Health Project (MCHP), which worked for ten years to change the lives of people in and around Battle Creek. This was a farming area with eight hundred one-room schools, many in poor condition, and almost no good libraries or medical care. MCHP provided additional education for doctors, nurses, teachers, ministers, social workers, newspaper editors, veterinarians, police chiefs, and school janitors. It created public health programs so that children could get dental care and be vaccinated against childhood diseases, and so that pregnant women could learn how to care for their babies. There were summer and winter camps for children from very poor homes. Sometimes skinny children gained 30 to 40 pounds at

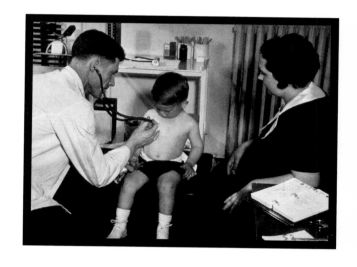

A child receives medical care as part of the Michigan Community Health Project.

camp, and when they came home, their parents did not recognize them!

In 1948, the 285,000 people of the seven counties affected by the project were so impressed by how MCHP improved their lives that they voted to tax themselves to keep the project going.

Building the Community... and Beyond

For the first twelve years of its existence, the W. K. Kellogg Foundation concentrated on helping the people of Michigan. In 1942, the U.S. Government asked the foundation to start agricultural and educational projects in Latin America. The foundation now helps people in many countries all over the world.

The foundation was able to extend its efforts to help people in Latin America because the Kellogg Company was so successful and grew fast. New

Today, the Kellogg Foundation supports programs all over the world, including helping these children receive an education in Brazil.

cereals, such as Shredded Wheat, 40% Bran Flakes, All-Bran®, and Rice Krispies® joined the original corn flakes on store shelves during the time that Kellogg ran the company.

Today, almost one hundred years after W. K. Kellogg began his own company, Kellogg's sells one of three of all cereal packages bought in the United States and one half of all cereal eaten in foreign countries.

Kellogg's sells cereals in 160 countries and has factories in 33 locations in 18 countries around the world. The company headquarters is still Battle Creek, where people watch sporting events in Kellogg Arena, hear concerts in Kellogg Auditorium, and land and take off from Kellogg Airport.

W. K. Kellogg died on October 6, 1951, at the age of 91. At the end of his life, W. K. was blind and lived quietly with a few helpers and a dog that he loved. When he died, he knew he had founded both a company and a foundation that are a major influence on the people of Michigan and people all over the world.

Kellogg in his later years with his dog

Battle Creek, Michigan

Battle Creek today is a city of slightly more than 53,000 people located in southwestern Michigan. Originally called "Health City," it is now know as "Cereal City." There is a cereal-themed attraction called Kellogg's Cereal City USA, where visitors can view exhibits on the history of cereal and Battle Creek, meet the characters featured on Kellogg's cereal boxes, and learn about health and nutrition. The city also holds an annual cereal festival featuring "The World's Longest Breakfast Table" in June.

Battle Creek

In Your Community

Kellogg's cereals are sold in 160 countries around the world. Where are they in your community? Look in the cereal cupboard in your kitchen. Are any cereals made by Kellogg?

Take a trip to the biggest supermarket in your community. Count the number of different products made by Kellogg. Kellogg owns Eggo Frozen Waffles® and Worthington Foods, so all the

Timeline

Seventh-day Adventists establish headquarters in Battle Creek near Kellogg home. This religion was an important influence on the Kellogg family, including W. K. Kellogg.

W. K. Kellogg goes to work for his brother Dr. John Harvey Kellogg at the Battle Creek Sanitarium.

W. K. founds the Battle Creek Toasted Corn Flake Company.

1856 — **1860** — **1880** — **1894** — **1906**

W. K. Kellogg born on April 7 in Battle Creek.

The Kellogg brothers invent the wheat flake at the Sanitas Food Company.

Kellogg's products will not be in the cereal section. Count how many non-Kellogg's cereals are in your store. Which is the bigger number-Kellogg's cereals or non-Kellogg's cereals?

Compare the nutrition information on the side panel for Kellogg's Rice Krispies® and Kellogg's Corn Flakes™. Which one do you think is better for your health?

Is there someone who has meant a lot to your community in the way Kellogg has to Battle Creek? Are the schools, parks, and airport named for anyone? Which company has the largest number of workers in your town? How does that company help your community?

1907
W. K.'s factory for the Battle Creek Toasted Corn Flake Company burns to the ground and then is immediately rebuilt.

1925
W. K. Kellogg gives the community of Battle Creek an auditorium, a junior high school, and a recreation center

1930
Kellogg establishes the W. K. Kellogg Foundation to help people, especially children, to improve themselves through education and health care.

1938
Michigan Community Health Project begins and improves the lives of more than a quarter of a million people in and around Battle Creek, Michigan.

1939
W. K. Kellogg retires as head of the Kellogg Company.

1951
After ten years of blindness and a few months of deteriorating health, W.K. Kellogg dies on October 6.

To Find Out More

Here are some additional resources to help you learn about W. K. Kellogg, nutrition, and Michigan:

Books

Butler, Mary, Frances Thornton, and Martin Ashley. *The Best to You Each Morning: W. K. Kellogg and Kellogg Company.* Heritage Publications, Historical Society of Battle Creek, 1995.

Fradin, Dennis Brindell. *Michigan.* Children's Press, 1996.

Kalbacken, Joan. *The Food Pyramid.* Children's Press, 1998.

Organizations and Online Sites

Kellogg Company
P.O. Box CAMB
Battle Creek, MI 49016
http://www.kelloggs.com/
Lively, colorful website that provides games, recipes, nutritional information, and a look inside the cereal factory.

Team Nutrition
http://www.fns.usda.gov/tn/Students/Kids/index.htm
Team Nutrition, a part of the U.S. Department of Agriculture, created this site for children to learn about nutrition and exercise. Includes games, recipes, fun facts, and links.

USDA for Kids
http://www.usda.gov/news/usdakids/index.html
This site, created by the U.S. Department of Agriculture, provides links to a wealth of information on health, nutrition, agriculture, and science.

W.K. Kellogg Foundation
One Michigan Avenue East
Battle Creek, MI 49017-4058
http://www.wkkf.org
Visit this site to learn more about how Kellogg through his foundation continues to help people. Includes photos, information, and links to different community programs.

Index

About the Author

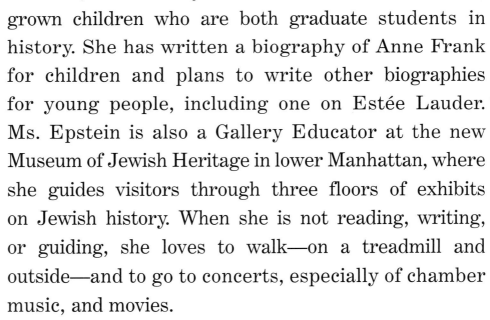

Rachel Epstein lives in Brooklyn Heights, just across the East River from Manhattan, with her husband, who is a lawyer. She has two grown children who are both graduate students in history. She has written a biography of Anne Frank for children and plans to write other biographies for young people, including one on Estée Lauder. Ms. Epstein is also a Gallery Educator at the new Museum of Jewish Heritage in lower Manhattan, where she guides visitors through three floors of exhibits on Jewish history. When she is not reading, writing, or guiding, she loves to walk—on a treadmill and outside—and to go to concerts, especially of chamber music, and movies.

When Ms. Epstein was growing up in Silver Spring, Maryland, the Battle Creek name she saw on her Corn Flakes box each morning seemed like a magical place.